9 Golden Rules Of Affiliate Marketing
AFFILIATE MARKETING FOR BEGINNERS

By Eli Rogers

2023 Edition

"Don't Count the Days, Make the Days Count!"

Foreword:

When it comes to affiliate marketing, persistence and patience are key traits that successful marketers possess. The path to success in affiliate marketing is rarely a straight line, and there will be ups and downs along the way. This can make it tempting to give up when things get tough, but quitting should not be an option.

One of the main benefits of affiliate marketing is that it allows marketers to build a passive income stream over time. This means that the efforts you put into your marketing today will continue to pay off for months or even years to come. However, building a successful affiliate marketing business takes time and effort, and it can be frustrating when progress seems slow.

The key to success in affiliate marketing is to stay focused and committed to your goals. This means that even when things get tough, you need to keep pushing forward and making progress. One of the ways to do this is by setting short-term goals for yourself and tracking your progress. This way, you can see the small wins along the way and stay motivated to keep going.

Another way to stay persistent and patient in affiliate marketing is to surround yourself with a supportive community. This could be a group of fellow affiliate marketers, or a coach or mentor who can offer guidance and support. Having a community of people who understand what you're going through and can offer encouragement can be a huge help when things get tough.

Finally, it's important to have a long-term perspective when it comes to affiliate marketing.

Success in affiliate marketing often comes in small increments, but over time these increments add up to significant progress. By staying focused, committed, and patient, you can achieve great things in affiliate marketing and build a successful, passive income stream.

You need to focus on staying persistent and patient, setting short-term goals, surrounding yourself with a supportive community, and having a long-term perspective. By doing these things, you can build a successful affiliate marketing business over time and enjoy the benefits of passive income for years to come.

Introduction:

How did I get introduced to affiliate marketing?

I was 18 years old and I just returned back home from a youth correctional facility. I was awarded to the state of Utah at 16 for my delinquent and juvenile decision making. Moving back home caused a real sense of discomfort.

Most of the people I grew up with were on their way to college, and trade schools, and I wanted to be a rapper. My original dream was to play professional Basketball in the NBA. After my music dreams and music dreams were unreachable, I got lucky and came across affiliate marketing for the first time. There were several YouTube creators at the time that preached that ClickBank.com was the way to change your life. I didn't understand it at the time, and ultimately left it alone.

Fast forward to today and I now generate millions of dollars from affiliate marketing. I hope you find this book informative and inspirational. Good luck on your journey.

Chapter 1: Choose Your Niche

Choosing a niche in affiliate marketing is one of the most important decisions an affiliate marketer can make. The niche you choose will determine the products you promote, the target audience you reach, and the overall success of your affiliate marketing efforts. In this section, we will discuss in depth why choosing a niche is valuable, and provide examples of some of the best niches for affiliate marketing.

The Importance of Choosing a Niche

1. Targeting a Specific Audience

One of the biggest advantages of choosing a niche in affiliate marketing is the ability to target a specific audience. By focusing on a specific area of interest, you can reach a group of people who are interested in the products or services you are promoting. This results in a more targeted and engaged audience, as opposed to a broad and unfocused audience.

For example, let's say you are interested in the health and wellness industry. By choosing this niche, you can focus on promoting health and wellness products, such as supplements, fitness equipment, and healthy food options. By targeting this specific audience, you can reach people who are interested in maintaining a healthy lifestyle and are more likely to purchase the products you are promoting.

This targeted approach can also result in higher conversion rates, as you are reaching a group of people who are more likely to be interested in the products you are promoting. Additionally, by targeting a specific audience, you can create a more personal connection with your audience, as you are able to understand their needs and provide information that is relevant to them.

2. Building Expertise

Another key benefit of choosing a niche in affiliate marketing is the ability to build expertise in a specific area. By focusing on a specific area of interest, you can gain a deeper understanding of the products and services you are promoting. This knowledge can help you provide valuable information to your audience and build trust with them. Additionally, you can use your expertise to create better and more informative content that will help you stand out as an expert in your field.

For example, if you are promoting health and wellness products, you can create blog posts that provide information on the benefits of different supplements, the best types of fitness equipment, and healthy food options. By providing valuable information to your audience, you can establish yourself as a credible source of information, and make it easier for you to connect with your target audience and persuade them to purchase the products you are promoting.

This expertise can also help you create better marketing campaigns, as you are able to understand the needs and desires of your target audience. For example, you may be able to identify specific pain points or challenges that your audience is facing, and create campaigns that address these issues and provide solutions.

3. Creating a Unique Brand

A third key benefit of choosing a niche in affiliate marketing is the ability to create a unique brand. By focusing on a specific area of interest, you can differentiate yourself from other affiliate marketers and create a brand that is unique and memorable. This can help you build a strong following and establish yourself as a leading expert in your niche.
For example, if you are promoting health and wellness products, you can create a brand that focuses on promoting a healthy and balanced lifestyle. You can use this brand to promote your blog, social media accounts, and other marketing materials. By creating a unique brand, you can build a strong following and establish yourself as a leading expert in the health and wellness industry.

Top Niches

1. Health and Wellness

The health and wellness industry is one of the largest and most profitable niches for affiliate marketers. This industry includes products such as supplements, fitness equipment, healthy food options, and more. There is a large and growing demand for these products, as people are becoming more health conscious and interested in maintaining a healthy lifestyle.

One of the benefits of the health and wellness niche is the diversity of products you can promote. For example, you can promote supplements, fitness equipment, healthy food options, and more. This allows you to reach a wide range of people who are interested in maintaining a healthy lifestyle, and to promote products that are relevant to their needs. Additionally, the health and wellness niche is an evergreen niche, meaning that there will always be a demand for these products. People will always be interested in maintaining a healthy lifestyle, and this niche will continue to grow and evolve over time.

2. Personal Finance

The personal finance niche is another popular and profitable niche for affiliate marketers. This niche includes products such as financial planning software, investment tools, and more. People are always looking for ways to improve their financial situation, and this niche allows you to reach a wide range of people who are interested in financial planning and investment.

One of the benefits of the personal finance niche is that it is a broad and diverse niche. You can choose to focus on specific areas of interest, such as budgeting, investing, or retirement planning, and you can reach a wide range of people who are interested in these topics. Additionally, the personal finance niche is an evergreen niche, meaning that there will always be a demand for these products.

3. Technology

The technology niche is another popular and lucrative niche for affiliate marketers. This niche includes products such as computers, smartphones, gaming systems, and more. There is a constant demand for new and innovative technology products, and this niche allows you to reach a wide range of people who are interested in technology and the latest gadgets.

One of the benefits of the technology niche is that it is constantly evolving. As new technology products are developed, you can promote the latest and greatest products and reach a new and growing audience. Additionally, the technology niche is broad and diverse, allowing you to focus on specific areas of interest, such as gaming, smartphones, or computers.

4. Beauty and Personal Care

The beauty and personal care niche is another popular and profitable niche for affiliate marketers. This niche includes products such as skincare products, hair care products, makeup, and more. There is a constant demand for these products, as people are always looking for ways to improve their appearance and feel good about themselves.
One of the benefits of the beauty and personal care niche is that it is a diverse and broad niche. You can choose to focus on specific areas of interest, such as skincare, hair care, or makeup, and you can reach a wide range of people who are interested in these topics. Additionally, the beauty and personal care niche is an evergreen niche, meaning that there will always be a demand for these products.

5. Home and Garden

The home and garden niche is another popular and profitable niche for affiliate marketers. This niche includes products such as home improvement tools, furniture, gardening equipment, and more. People are always looking for ways to improve their homes and gardens, and this niche allows you to reach a wide range of people who are interested in these topics.

One of the benefits of the home and garden niche is that it is an evergreen niche, meaning that there will always be a demand for these products. Additionally, the home and garden niche is diverse, allowing you to focus on specific areas of interest, such as home improvement, furniture, or gardening.

Another benefit of the home and garden niche is that it is a relatively low-competition niche, meaning that there is less competition for keywords and for promoting products. This makes it easier for you to establish your brand and reach a targeted audience, and it also means that you can potentially earn a higher commission on your sales.

6. Pet Care

The pet care niche is another popular and profitable niche for affiliate marketers. This niche includes products such as pet food, pet toys, pet grooming supplies, and more. People are passionate about their pets and are always looking for ways to improve their care and well-being.

One of the benefits of the pet care niche is that it is a diverse and broad niche, allowing you to focus on specific areas of interest, such as dog care, cat care, or bird care. Additionally, the pet care niche is an evergreen niche, meaning that there will always be a demand for these products.

Another benefit of the pet care niche is that people are passionate about their pets and are willing to spend money on them. This means that they are more likely to make a purchase, and that you can earn a higher commission on your sales.

7. Travel

The travel niche is another popular and profitable niche for affiliate marketers. This niche includes products such as travel gear, travel guides, and more. People are always interested in exploring new destinations and experiencing new cultures, and this niche allows you to reach a wide range of people who are interested in travel.

One of the benefits of the travel niche is that it is a broad and diverse niche, allowing you to focus on specific areas of interest, such as budget travel, luxury travel, or adventure travel. Additionally, the travel niche is an evergreen niche, meaning that there will always be a demand for these products.

Another benefit of the travel niche is that people are often looking for inspiration and advice when planning their travels, and they are more likely to make a purchase if they feel that they are getting valuable information and guidance. By providing valuable content and recommendations, you can build trust with your audience and increase your chances of making a sale.

8. Personal Development

The personal development niche is another popular and profitable niche for affiliate marketers. This niche includes products such as self-help books, courses, and more. People are always looking for ways to improve themselves and achieve their goals, and this niche allows you to reach a wide range of people who are interested in personal development.

One of the benefits of the personal development niche is that it is a broad and diverse niche, allowing you to focus on specific areas of interest, such as personal finance, relationship advice, or career development. Additionally, the personal development niche is an evergreen niche, meaning that there will always be a demand for these products.

Another benefit of the personal development niche is that people are often looking for guidance and support when trying to achieve their goals, and they are more likely to make a purchase if it increases your chances of making a sale.

Chapter 2: Partner With Reputable Brands/Companies

Choosing the right brands to partner with in affiliate marketing is crucial to the success of your business. The right brands can help you establish trust and credibility with your audience, increase your earnings, and provide you with the support and resources you need to succeed.

On the other hand, partnering with the wrong brands can harm your reputation and result in poor sales, making it difficult for you to achieve long-term success in affiliate marketing.

There are several key factors to consider when choosing the right brands to partner with in affiliate marketing. Firstly, it is important to choose brands that are reputable and well-established. These brands are more likely to provide high-quality products, offer higher affiliate commissions, and provide reliable affiliate support. Additionally, reputable brands are also more likely to provide access to high-quality marketing materials, which can help you promote their products more effectively.

Another factor to consider when choosing brands to partner with is the alignment of their products and values with your own. Partnering with brands whose products align with your niche and values can help you build a more authentic and credible affiliate marketing business. For example, if you are a health and wellness blogger, you may choose to partner with brands that offer natural and organic products, as this aligns with your values and niche.

It is also important to consider the size and reach of the brands you partner with. Larger brands with a wider reach may be more likely to generate more sales and revenue, as they have the resources and marketing power to reach a larger audience. However, smaller and niche brands may also be a good option, as they may offer more targeted products that align with your niche, and may also offer higher affiliate commissions.

Ultimately, choosing the right brands to partner with in affiliate marketing is a balance between considering the reputation, product alignment, size, and reach of the brands, as well as your own goals and objectives as an affiliate marketer. By taking the time to research and carefully consider the brands you partner with, you can ensure that your affiliate marketing business is successful and sustainable in the long term.

1. Increased Trust and Credibility

One of the most important benefits of partnering with reputable companies is that it can increase your own trust and credibility with your audience. When you promote products from well-established companies, your audience is more likely to trust that the products are high-quality and reliable. Additionally, promoting products from reputable companies can help you establish yourself as an expert in your niche, which can increase your credibility and help you build a loyal following.

2. Improved Product Quality

Another important benefit of partnering with reputable companies is that the products you promote are more likely to be of high quality. Reputable companies are more likely to invest in product development and quality control, which can result in better products for your audience. This can not only lead to increased customer satisfaction, but can also increase the likelihood of repeat purchases, which can help you generate long-term revenue.

3. Increased Affiliate Commission

Partnering with reputable companies can also increase your potential earnings as an affiliate. Many reputable companies offer higher affiliate commissions than smaller or less established companies. Additionally, reputable companies may offer other benefits, such as bonuses and incentives, which can increase your earnings even further. By choosing to promote products from reputable companies, you can increase your potential earnings and maximize your return on investment.

4. Reliable Affiliate Support

Working with reputable companies can also provide you with reliable affiliate support. Reputable companies are more likely to have dedicated affiliate support teams that can provide you with assistance when you need it. This can include help with marketing materials, technical support, and more. Additionally, reputable companies may also provide access to training and educational resources, which can help you improve your skills as an affiliate marketer.

5. Better Marketing Materials

Reputable companies are also more likely to provide high-quality marketing materials that can help you promote their products. This can include product images, videos, and descriptions, as well as email templates and social media content. Having access to these materials can make it easier for you to promote the products and generate sales, and can help you build a more professional and effective affiliate marketing business.

6. Increased Consumer Confidence

When you promote products from reputable companies, you can also increase consumer confidence in the products you are promoting. Consumers are more likely to trust products from reputable companies, and may be more likely to make a purchase based on your recommendation. Additionally, promoting products from reputable companies can help you establish yourself as a trustworthy and credible affiliate, which can help you build a loyal following and increase your long-term success as an affiliate marketer.

7. Increased Product Longevity

Another important benefit of partnering with reputable companies is that the products you promote are more likely to have a long lifespan. Reputable companies are more likely to invest in research and development, which can result in products that are more durable and have a longer lifespan. This can help you generate long-term revenue, as your audience may be more likely to make repeat purchases in the future.

Chapter 3: Build A Target Audience

Building a target audience is one of the most important steps in any successful marketing strategy, including affiliate marketing. Having a clear understanding of your target audience allows you to tailor your marketing efforts and messaging to better meet their needs and interests, increasing the likelihood that they will engage with your content and ultimately make a purchase through your affiliate links.

In affiliate marketing, building a target audience begins with identifying your niche. Your niche is the specific area of interest or product category that you will be promoting as an affiliate marketer. Once you have established your niche, you can then begin to research and understand your target audience, including their demographics, interests, and purchasing habits.

One effective way to build a target audience is to create buyer personas. Buyer personas are fictional characters that represent your ideal customer, and they are created by combining research and data about your target audience with insights and information about their behavior and motivations. Creating buyer personas allows you to better understand your target audience and develop a clear picture of who they are, what they want, and how they behave.

Another important aspect of building a target audience is understanding their pain points and needs. This information can be used to tailor your marketing messaging and approach, making it more relevant and appealing to your target audience. For example, if your target audience is primarily interested in natural and organic products, your messaging should focus on the health and wellness benefits of these products, rather than their cost savings.

In addition to researching your target audience, it is also important to engage with them and build relationships. This can be done through a variety of methods, including social media, email marketing, and content marketing. By actively engaging with your target audience and building relationships, you can establish trust and credibility with them, and position yourself as a valuable resource in your niche.

Finally, it is important to continually monitor and analyze your target audience to ensure that your marketing efforts are aligned with their changing needs and interests. This can be done by tracking metrics such as website traffic, engagement rates, and conversion rates, as well as through regular communication and feedback from your audience.

In conclusion, building a target audience is a critical component of a successful affiliate marketing strategy. By taking the time to understand and engage with your target audience, you can develop a more targeted and effective marketing approach, and increase the likelihood of success for your affiliate marketing business.

In this example, we will walk through a step-by-step process for building a target audience for an affiliate marketing business focused on promoting healthy and natural lifestyle products.

Step 1: Define Your Niche

The first step in building a target audience is to define your niche. For this example, we will assume that our niche is healthy and natural lifestyle products. This includes a wide range of products such as natural beauty and skincare products, organic food and supplements, and eco-friendly household products.

Step 2: Conduct Market Research

The next step is to conduct market research to gain a better understanding of your target audience. This can be done through a variety of methods, including online surveys, focus groups, and competitor analysis. During this stage, it is important to gather information about your target audience's demographics, interests, behaviors, and pain points.

Step 3: Create Buyer Personas

Once you have gathered your research, the next step is to create buyer personas. Buyer personas are fictional characters that represent your ideal customer, and they are created by combining research and data about your target audience with insights and information about their behavior and motivations. For our example, we will create two buyer personas for our target audience:

1. "Sophie," a 32-year-old working mother who is interested in natural and organic products for herself and her family.

She is motivated by health and wellness and is looking for products that are affordable and easily accessible.

2. "Jake," a 40-year-old health-conscious man who is interested in natural and organic supplements to support his active lifestyle. He is willing to pay a premium for high-quality products and is an avid reader of health and wellness blogs.

Step 4: Identify Your Target Audience's Pain Points and Needs

Next, it is important to understand your target audience's pain points and needs. For our example, we can use the information gathered in our market research to determine that our target audience is motivated by health and wellness and is looking for affordable, high-quality products that are easily accessible.

Step 5: Engage with Your Target Audience through Social Media

Social media is a powerful tool for building relationships with your target audience. By actively engaging with your target audience on social media, you can build trust and credibility with them, and position yourself as a valuable resource in your niche. To engage with your target audience, you can use a variety of strategies, including:

1. Creating and sharing relevant and valuable content, such as blog posts and videos, that addresses their pain points and interests.
2. Interacting with your target audience by responding to comments and messages, and asking for feedback and suggestions.
3. Running social media contests and promotions to increase engagement and drive traffic to your website.

Step 6: Use Email Marketing to Build Relationships

In addition to social media, email marketing is also a powerful tool for building relationships with your target audience. By collecting email addresses from your website visitors and social media followers, you can send regular emails to your target audience to keep them engaged and updated on your latest promotions and offerings.

Step 7: Track and Analyze Your Results

Finally, it is important to track and analyze your results to ensure that your marketing efforts are aligned with your target audience's changing needs and interests. This can be done by tracking metrics such as website traffic, engagement, conversion rates, and customer feedback. Based on your analysis, you can make informed decisions about what changes to make to your marketing strategy to better meet the needs of your target audience and drive more sales.

By following these steps, you can build a strong and engaged target audience for your affiliate marketing business. By taking the time to understand your target audience and their needs, you can tailor your marketing efforts to better meet their needs, increase engagement, and ultimately drive more sales through your affiliate links.

In conclusion, building a target audience is an ongoing process that requires dedication, effort, and a willingness to adapt and evolve based on your target audience's changing needs and interests. By following the steps outlined above and using tools such as social media and email marketing, you can build a strong and engaged target audience that will help drive the success of your affiliate marketing business.

Chapter 4: Offering Value

Affiliate marketing is a marketing strategy that involves promoting another company's products or services and earning a commission on any resulting sales. The key to success in affiliate marketing is offering value to your audience. When people feel that they are getting valuable information or services from you, they are more likely to trust you and make a purchase through your affiliate links.

To offer value in affiliate marketing, start by understanding your target audience. What are their needs and wants? What kind of information do they want to know about the products you are promoting? When you understand your audience, you can create content that is relevant and valuable to them. This can include blog posts, reviews, tutorials, and more.

It's also important to be transparent about your affiliate relationships. Let your audience know that you are an affiliate and that you may receive a commission for any sales made through your affiliate links. This will help build trust and credibility with your audience, making them more likely to make a purchase through your links.

Another way to offer value in affiliate marketing is by providing exclusive discounts or promotions to your audience. This can be a great incentive for people to make a purchase through your links, and it can also help you stand out from other affiliates promoting the same products.

Another key element to offering value in affiliate marketing is to focus on quality over quantity. Don't just promote any product or service just because you can earn a commission on it. Instead, choose products and services that you believe in and that align with your values and interests. When you promote products that you are passionate about, your audience will be able to see that and they will be more likely to trust your recommendations.

Finally, it's important to provide ongoing value to your audience. This can include creating more content related to the products you are promoting, answering questions, and providing helpful tips and tricks. When your audience sees that you are always looking for ways to help them, they will be more likely to continue to engage with your content and make purchases through your affiliate links.

In conclusion, offering value in affiliate marketing is essential to building a successful affiliate marketing business. When you provide valuable information, exclusive discounts, and ongoing support, your audience will be more likely to trust you and make a purchase through your affiliate links. By focusing on quality over quantity, being transparent about your affiliate relationships, and always looking for ways to help your audience, you can build a strong reputation and a successful affiliate marketing business.

The 5 steps for picking a product that offers value in affiliate marketing.

1. Consider the target audience: Before you select a product to promote, it's essential to know your target audience. The more you understand about their needs,

wants, and interests, the easier it will be to choose a product that offers value to them. To research your target audience, you can use surveys, focus groups, and online tools like Google Analytics.

2. Look for products that solve a problem: Products that solve a problem for your target audience are likely to offer value and be in high demand. For example, if your target audience is pet owners, you might consider promoting a pet training product that helps solve common behavior issues.

3. Check for product quality: High-quality products are likely to offer more value to your target audience, as they are more likely to provide a positive user experience and generate repeat sales. You can research the product's quality by reading reviews and testimonials from existing customers, and checking the company's return policy.

4. Consider the commission structure: When selecting a product to promote, it's important to consider the commission structure. Some affiliate programs offer a higher commission rate, which can make the product more valuable to promote. You should also consider the frequency of commission payouts and any bonuses or incentives that may be available.

5. Evaluate the market competition: It's essential to research the competition when choosing a product to promote. If the market is saturated with similar products, it may be more challenging to promote the product effectively. On the other hand, if there is limited competition, it may be easier to stand out and offer value to your target audience.

Example: One example of a product that fits the criteria of being a valuable affiliate product is a high-quality mattress. Mattresses are a necessary item for most people, and choosing the right one can be a significant investment. By promoting a high-quality mattress, you can offer value to your target audience by helping them find a product that will improve their sleep and overall quality of life. Additionally, mattresses have a long lifespan, meaning that customers are likely to make repeat purchases, providing a steady source of income for the affiliate.

To promote a high quality mattress effectively, there are several strategies that you can use. Here are five effective methods:

1. Develop targeted content: Create content that speaks directly to the target audience for your mattress. This can be in the form of blog posts, articles, videos, or infographics. The content should educate the audience

about the benefits of the mattress, how it differs from other products on the market, and why it is worth the investment.

2. Leverage social media: Use social media platforms such as Facebook, Twitter, Instagram, and LinkedIn to promote the mattress. Share informative and visually appealing posts that highlight the benefits of the mattress. You can also use social media advertising to target specific audiences and drive more traffic to your website.

3. Collaborate with influencers: Partner with influencers in the sleep and wellness space to help promote the mattress. These individuals have a large following and can help spread the word about your product. Consider offering influencers a commission or other incentives to promote your mattress.

4. Optimize your website: Make sure your website is optimized for search engines and provides a positive user experience. Use keywords related to the mattress in your website content, and ensure that all product pages are well-designed and easy to navigate.

5. Offer promotions and discounts: Running promotions and discounts can help incentivize people to make a purchase. Consider offering a discount on the mattress

or a bundle deal that includes accessories such as sheets and pillows. These promotions can help attract new customers and increase sales.

Chapter 5 - Optimize Your Website For Search Engines

Optimizing your website for search engines, commonly referred to as SEO, can bring many benefits to your website and your overall online presence. SEO involves making changes to your website and its content to improve its visibility and ranking on search engines such as Google, Bing, and Yahoo. By optimizing your website, you can attract more organic traffic to your site, which can lead to increased brand visibility, credibility, and authority.

Here are some of the benefits of optimizing your website with SEO:

1. Increased traffic: By improving your website's visibility on search engines, you can attract more organic traffic to your site, which can lead to increased sales and conversions. By optimizing your website, you can ensure that it appears at the top of the search engine results pages (SERPs) for keywords related to your niche or industry.

2. Better user experience: SEO optimization involves making changes to your website's design and content to ensure that it is user-friendly and easy to navigate. By improving your website's user experience, you can provide a better experience for your visitors, which can lead to increased engagement and conversions.

3. Improved brand visibility and credibility: By appearing at the top of the search engine results pages, you can improve your brand visibility and credibility. People are more likely to trust and engage with websites that appear at the top of the search engine results pages, as they are seen as more authoritative and credible.

4. Increased brand authority: By providing high-quality, relevant content on your website, you can establish your brand as an authority in your niche or industry. This can lead to increased brand recognition, trust, and loyalty, which can result in increased sales and conversions.

5. Better return on investment (ROI): SEO optimization can be a cost-effective way to attract traffic to your website, as it involves making changes to your website's design and content rather than relying on paid advertising. By improving your website's visibility and ranking on search engines, you can see a better return on investment (ROI) from your marketing efforts.

Overall, optimizing your website for search engines can bring many benefits to your website and your online presence. By improving your website's visibility and ranking on search engines, you can attract more organic traffic to your site, improve your brand visibility and credibility, establish your brand as an authority in your niche or industry, and see a better return on investment (ROI) from your marketing efforts.

Now that we understand the benefits of optimizing websites, we now have to ask how do we accomplish this task? Let's look at how you would go about optimizing your website.

1. Keyword research: Start by researching the keywords and phrases that your target audience is likely to use when searching for a high-quality mattress. Make a list of these keywords and use them in your website's content, meta tags, and other relevant areas. This will help search engines understand what your website is about and improve its chances of ranking higher in search results for those keywords.

2. On-page optimization: Ensure that your website is well-structured and that its pages are optimized for both search engines and users. This includes using descriptive and meaningful page titles, meta descriptions, and headings, as well as using relevant and high-quality images and videos. Additionally, make sure that your

website is easy to navigate and that its pages load quickly.

3. Content creation: Creating high-quality, original, and informative content that is relevant to your target audience is essential for SEO. Use keywords naturally in your content and provide value to your audience by answering their questions and addressing their concerns. Also, make sure to regularly update your content to keep it fresh and relevant.

4. Link building: Building high-quality links to your website from other relevant websites can greatly improve its search engine rankings. This is because search engines use links to determine the relevance and authority of a website. Focus on building relationships with other websites in your niche and obtaining links through guest posting, creating valuable content, and participating in online forums and communities.

5. Technical SEO: Make sure that your website is technically sound and that it meets best practices for SEO. This includes having a mobile-friendly website, using SSL encryption, and using a clean and well-structured URL structure. Additionally, make sure that your website is free of broken links, errors, and other technical issues that can negatively impact its search engine rankings.

By focusing on these key elements, you can optimize your website for search engines and improve its ranking in search engine results pages, which can help you grow your affiliate marketing business and increase your earnings.

Chapter 6 - Use Social Proof

Social proof is a powerful concept in affiliate marketing that can help you build trust with your audience, increase conversions, and grow your business. In this comprehensive guide, we'll explore the concept of social proof in depth and provide you with practical tips on how to leverage it effectively in your affiliate marketing efforts.

What is social proof?
Social proof is a psychological phenomenon where people tend to follow the actions of others in an attempt to conform to what is perceived as normal behavior. In other words, if a large number of people are doing something, others are more likely to follow suit.

In the context of affiliate marketing, social proof refers to the use of endorsements, testimonials, and customer reviews to build credibility and trust with potential customers. Social proof can be in the form of stars, ratings, or numerical ratings.

Why is social proof important in affiliate marketing?

Social proof is an important component of successful affiliate marketing because it can have a significant impact on consumer behavior. By providing evidence of the quality and value of a product or service, social proof can help overcome skepticism and increase the likelihood of a conversion.

For example, if a potential customer sees that hundreds of other customers have purchased and highly rated a product, they are more likely to trust that the product is of high quality and purchase it themselves.

Additionally, social proof can help you establish credibility and build trust with your audience. By providing real-life examples of the value and benefits of a product or service, you can demonstrate that it has been successfully used by others and is worth their consideration.

How to leverage social proof in affiliate marketing

There are several ways to leverage social proof in affiliate marketing, including:

1. Customer reviews and ratings

One of the most effective forms of social proof is customer reviews and ratings. By showcasing real customer experiences and opinions, you can provide valuable insights into the quality and value of a product or service.

To make the most of customer reviews and ratings, it's important to display them prominently on your website or product pages. This can be done through the use of product rating stars, customer testimonials, or even video reviews.

2. Social media engagement

Another way to leverage social proof is through social media engagement. By showcasing the number of likes, followers, and comments you have on your social media channels, you can demonstrate the popularity and reach of your brand.

For example, if you have a large following on Instagram, you can showcase this on your website or product pages to increase credibility and trust with potential customers.

3. Influencer marketing

Influencer marketing is a form of affiliate marketing that involves partnering with popular and influential individuals in your niche to promote products or services. By leveraging the reach and credibility of influencers, you can tap into the power of social proof to increase conversions and grow your business.

For example, if a popular beauty influencer posts a review of a new skincare product and raves about its benefits, this is likely to have a significant impact on the product's popularity and sales.

4. Case studies and success stories

Case studies and success stories are a powerful form of social proof that can help you demonstrate the value and benefits of a product or service. By showcasing real-life examples of people who have successfully used a product or service, you can build credibility and trust with potential customers. For example, if you have a case study that highlights the success of a customer who used a particular product to solve a specific problem, this is likely to have a significant impact on the product's popularity and sales.

Chapter 7 - Test & Analyze

Testing and analyzing are critical components of effective affiliate marketing. They provide insights into the performance of your campaigns, and allow you to make data-driven decisions to optimize your marketing efforts and improve your results.

One of the key benefits of testing and analyzing is that it allows you to identify what is working well and what is not. By tracking metrics such as click-through rate (CTR), conversion rate, and return on investment (ROI), you can determine the effectiveness of your campaigns and make adjustments accordingly.

For example, if you notice that one ad is performing better than others, you can replicate its success by incorporating similar elements into your other ads. On the other hand, if you see that a certain landing page is underperforming, you can make changes to improve its conversion rate.

Testing and analyzing also enable you to optimize your customer journey. By understanding the customer journey, you can identify where customers are dropping off and make changes to improve their experience. For example, you may find that a high percentage of visitors are leaving your site after viewing a specific product page. This could indicate that the page is not providing enough information or is not compelling enough to entice visitors to make a purchase. By testing different versions of the page, you can determine which elements are most effective in driving conversions.

Another benefit of testing and analyzing is that it allows you to improve your targeting. By analyzing your audience data, you can identify your most valuable customers and target them more effectively with your marketing efforts. For example, if you notice that a certain group of customers are more likely to purchase after clicking on a certain type of ad, you can prioritize that type of ad for that group.

Ways to accomplish testing and analyzing in affiliate marketing include A/B testing, multivariate testing, and split testing. A/B testing involves creating two versions of a landing page or ad and testing them with a portion of your audience to determine which version performs better.

Multivariate testing allows you to test multiple elements of a landing page or ad at the same time, such as the headline, images, and call to action. Split testing involves randomly dividing your audience into two or more groups and testing different elements of your marketing efforts with each group. To summarize, testing and analyzing are essential components of effective affiliate marketing. By testing and analyzing your campaigns, you can identify what is working well, optimize your customer journey, improve your targeting, and ultimately drive better results for your business.

Let's take a look at an in-depth example of testing and analyzing in affiliate marketing:

Imagine you are promoting a product called "GymGo Pro," a fitness app that helps people track their workouts and progress. In order to see if your promotion efforts are effective, it is crucial to test and analyze different aspects of your affiliate marketing strategy.

One way to test and analyze is by using A/B testing on your landing pages. You can create two versions of your landing page, each with a different headline or call-to-action, and then use a tool like Google Optimize to determine which version performs better. For example, you might test a headline that says "Get Fit with GymGo Pro" against one that says "Transform Your Workouts with GymGo Pro." By analyzing the data, you can see which headline is more effective in driving conversions and use that information to optimize your landing page for maximum results.

Another way to test and analyze is by tracking your affiliate links. You can use a tool like Pretty Links to track clicks and conversions on your affiliate links. This will allow you to see which sources of traffic are driving the most sales, and you can use that information to focus your efforts on the most effective channels. For example, you might see that your social media posts are driving a lot of conversions, so you can focus more of your time and resources on that channel.

Finally, you can also use analytics tools like Google Analytics to see how people are interacting with your website and how long they are staying on your pages. This will help you identify any issues with your website design or navigation that might be hindering conversions. For example, if you see that people are leaving your site quickly, you might need to improve the user experience or add more information about the product.

Testing and analyzing is an important part of affiliate marketing because it helps you understand what is working and what is not, and you can use that information to optimize your strategy for maximum results. By using data and insights to drive your decisions, you can increase your chances of success and make more money as an affiliate marketer.

Chapter 8 - Stay Up To Date

Staying up to date in affiliate marketing is essential for several reasons:

1. Stay Ahead of Competition: The affiliate marketing industry is highly competitive, and new players are entering the market every day. To stay ahead of the competition, it's important to stay up to date with the latest trends and best practices in the industry. This will help you identify new opportunities and find ways to differentiate yourself from your competitors.

2. Keep up with Algorithm Updates: Search engines like Google regularly update their algorithms, and these updates can have a significant impact on your website's ranking and visibility. Staying up to date with these changes will help you ensure that your website is

optimized for search engines and that you're not missing out on any opportunities to improve your ranking.

3. Adapt to New Technologies: Technology is constantly evolving, and affiliate marketers must stay on top of new technologies to remain competitive. For example, mobile optimization has become increasingly important in recent years, and it's crucial for affiliate marketers to ensure that their websites are mobile-friendly to reach a wider audience.

4. Stay Ahead of Regulations: The affiliate marketing industry is regulated, and new laws and regulations are introduced from time to time. It's important to stay up to date with these regulations to ensure that your marketing activities are in compliance with the law. Failure to comply with regulations can result in fines and legal action, which can be damaging to your reputation and business.

5. Leverage New Marketing Channels: Affiliate marketing is constantly evolving, and new marketing channels are emerging all the time. For example, social media platforms like Instagram and TikTok have become popular marketing channels in recent years, and affiliate marketers who are up to date with these channels have the opportunity to reach new audiences and drive more sales.

6. Improve Your Skills: The affiliate marketing industry is highly dynamic, and new techniques and strategies are emerging all the time. By staying up to date with these developments, you'll be able to improve your skills and knowledge, which will help you to achieve better results and grow your business.

7. Stay Relevant: Finally, staying up to date in affiliate marketing will help you stay relevant and current in the minds of your audience. By being aware of the latest trends and developments in the industry, you'll be able to create content and campaigns that are relevant and appealing to your target audience.

Staying organized and up to date is essential in affiliate marketing to ensure success and growth. There are several tools and systems that can help you in this regard. Some of the best include:

1. Project Management Tools: Tools like Asana, Trello, or Monday can help you manage tasks, deadlines, and communication with team members.
2. CRM Software: Customer Relationship Management (CRM) software like Hubspot or Salesforce can help you manage and track customer interactions, which is essential for affiliate marketing.

3. Email Marketing Tools: Tools like Mailchimp or Convertkit can help you manage your email list, create and send newsletters, and track the success of your email campaigns.
4. Analytics Tools: Tools like Google Analytics can help you track your website traffic, conversions, and the success of your campaigns.
5. Keyword Research Tools: Tools like Ahrefs, Moz, or SEMrush can help you research keywords, monitor your rankings, and track your competition.
6. Social Media Management Tools: Tools like Hootsuite, Buffer, or Later can help you manage multiple social media accounts, schedule posts, and track the success of your social media campaigns.

Each tool has its own strengths and weaknesses, so it's important to consider your specific needs and budget when choosing the best system or tool for staying organized and up to date in affiliate marketing. Failing to stay up to date in affiliate marketing can have a bad impact as well, let's take a look at negative consequences. Some of these include:

1. Outdated marketing techniques: If you're not staying up to date, you may be using outdated marketing techniques that are no longer effective. This can lead to poor results and a decline in sales.

2. Lost opportunities: The affiliate marketing landscape is constantly evolving, and new opportunities are always emerging. If you're not staying up to date, you may miss out on these opportunities and be left behind by your competition.

3. Uninformed decision making: Without staying up to date, you may not have the most accurate information and data to make informed decisions about your affiliate marketing strategy. This can lead to ineffective campaigns and decreased profits.

4. Lack of compliance: Affiliate marketing regulations and guidelines can change frequently. If you're not staying up to date, you may end up breaking these regulations and facing consequences such as fines or legal action.

In conclusion, staying up to date in affiliate marketing is essential for success. It will help you stay ahead of the competition, adapt to new technologies and regulations, leverage new marketing channels, improve your skills, and stay relevant to your target audience. To stay up to date in affiliate marketing, it's important to regularly read industry news and blogs, attend events and conferences, and participate in online forums and communities.

Chapter 9 - Persistence And Patience

The essence of persistence and patience in affiliate marketing can be best understood by examining why these qualities are so important to success in this industry. Essentially, affiliate marketing is a long-term business that requires a great deal of hard work and dedication in order to succeed. This means that marketers must be willing to put in the time and effort to build their businesses and create a steady stream of income over time.

One of the biggest challenges in affiliate marketing is staying focused and motivated over the long term. The internet is full of distractions and competing priorities, and it can be easy to lose sight of your goals if you're not careful. This is why persistence and patience are so important. Marketers who are able to stay focused and keep pushing forward, even when they face challenges and obstacles, are much more likely to achieve success in the long run.

Another important factor to consider is that affiliate marketing is a highly competitive industry. There are thousands of other marketers out there, all vying for the same target audience and trying to make a living through affiliate marketing. This means that success is not guaranteed, and that you may have to try many different strategies and approaches before you find something that works for you. This is why persistence and patience are so important, as you may need to keep trying and experimenting for a long time before you see real results.

It's also important to understand that affiliate marketing is a constantly evolving industry. New trends and technologies are emerging all the time, and it's important to stay up-to-date with these developments in order to remain competitive. This can be a challenge, as it requires a great deal of time and effort to stay informed and to keep learning new skills and techniques. However, those who are persistent and patient will be able to stay ahead of the curve and to continue to grow their businesses over time.

here are several reasons why persistence and patience are essential in affiliate marketing:

1. Building Trust: One of the most important aspects of affiliate marketing is building trust with your audience. This takes time, as you must consistently deliver valuable content and promotions to your followers. Over time, your followers will come to see you as a trusted authority in your niche, and they will be more likely to make purchases through your affiliate links.

2. Finding the Right Products: There are many products and services that you can promote as an affiliate marketer. It is important to take your time and find the right products that fit your niche and your audience. This may require some trial and error, as you test different

products and promotions to see what resonates with your audience.

3. Learning from Mistakes: Affiliate marketing is a complex and ever-changing field, and it is inevitable that you will make mistakes along the way. However, it is important to learn from these mistakes and to persist in your efforts to improve your skills and strategies. Over time, you will become a more effective affiliate marketer as you learn from your experiences.

4. Building Traffic and Conversion Rates: One of the biggest challenges in affiliate marketing is driving traffic to your website and converting that traffic into sales. This takes time and persistence, as you work to optimize your website, create valuable content, and promote your products and services effectively.

5. Growing Your Network: Affiliate marketing is a highly competitive field, and it is important to build relationships with other affiliate marketers and industry experts. This can help you to stay up-to-date on the latest trends and strategies, and it can also help you to promote your products and services more effectively.

www.ingramcontent.com/pod-product-compliance
Lightning Source LLC
Chambersburg PA
CBHW062011220526
45467CB00032BA/2730